Inflation Proof: 8 Smart Strategies to Keep Your Wallet Full

Inflation Proof

Legal Notice:- This book is for informational purposes only. While every attempt has been made to verify the information provided in this book, neither the author nor the distributor assume any responsibility for errors or omissions. Any slights of people or organizations are unintentional and the Development of this book is bona fide. This book has been distributed with the understanding that we are not engaged in rendering technical, legal, accounting or other professional advice. In no event will the author and/or marketer be liable for any direct, indirect, incidental, consequential or other loss or damage arising out of the use of this document by any person, regardless of whether or not informed of the possibility of damages in advance.

Copyright © 2024 JWH Jr.

Table of Contents

Inflation Proof: 8 Smart Strategies to Keep Your Wallet Full.. 1

    Introduction:.. 7

    Inflation Proof: 8 Smart Strategies to Keep Your Wallet Full... 8

    Chapter 1:... 11

    Understanding Inflation: What It Is and Why It Matters... 11

        A Brief History of Inflation...................................... 11

        What Causes Inflation?... 12

        The Effects of Inflation... 14

        How to Measure Inflation...................................... 14

        Conclusion.. 15

    Chapter 2:... 15

    Budgeting Basics: The First Step to Beating Inflation 16

        What is a Budget?... 16

        Setting Up Your Budget... 17

            1. Assess Your Income.. 17

            2. Track Your Expenses...................................... 17

            3. Set Financial Goals... 18

4. Create Your Budget...18
Common Budgeting Methods................................19
Tips for Sticking to Your Budget..........................20
Making Adjustments in Inflationary Times............21
Conclusion..22
Chapter 3:..22
Smart Investing: Growing Your Money, Even When Prices Rise..22
Why Invest?..23
Types of Investments...23
Setting Investment Goals....................................25
Risk Tolerance...25
Diversification: Your Best Friend.........................26
Investing During Inflation..................................26
How to Start Investing.......................................27
Costs of Investing..28
Staying the Course...28
Conclusion..29
Chapter 4:..29
Haggling and Negotiation: Getting More for Less.....29
Understanding the Art of Haggling.......................30
Preparing to Negotiate......................................31

Strategies for Successful Negotiation...................31

Negotiating in Different Settings...........................33

Practicing Your Skills...34

Conclusion..35

Chapter 5:..35

DIY Solutions: Cutting Costs With Your Skills...........35

What is DIY?...36

Why DIY?..36

Popular DIY Projects...37

   1. Home Repairs..37

   2. Gardening..38

   3. Upcycling Furniture..38

   4. Homemade Cleaning Products.......................39

   5. Crafting Gifts..39

How to Get Started with DIY.................................39

Tips for Successful DIY...40

Resources for DIY...41

Conclusion..42

Chapter 6:..43

Saving Wisely: Where to Put Your Money Amid Inflation...43

The Importance of Saving.....................................43

Types of Savings Accounts......................................44
    1. Regular Savings Account................................44
    2. High-Yield Savings Account...........................44
    3. Money Market Accounts................................45
    4. Certificates of Deposit (CDs)........................45
Building an Emergency Fund................................46
Smart Saving Strategies......................................47
Staying Informed About Interest Rates..................48
Conclusion..49

Chapter 7:..49

Income Diversification: Finding Extra Dollars in Unexpected Places..50
What is Income Diversification?............................50
Why is Income Diversification Important?..............51
Exploring Income Diversification Options..............52
    1. Side Hustles..52
    2. Passive Income Sources................................53
    3. Starting a Small Business..............................54
    4. Investing in Your Education and Skills............54
Tips for Successfully Diversifying Your Income......54
Conclusion..56

Chapter 8:..57

Staying Informed: Keeping Up with Economic Trends 57
   The Importance of Staying Informed 57
   How to Stay Informed About Economic Trends 58
   Making Sense of Information 60
   Conclusion 61

Introduction:

Inflation Proof: 8 Smart Strategies to Keep Your Wallet Full

Picture this: You walk into your favorite grocery store, ready to grab your usual goodies, only to be struck by a frightening reality. The cereal you always buy is suddenly a dollar more. The milk costs an extra 50 cents, and even the bread has hiked up in price. You stand there, confused, wondering why everything seems to be getting more expensive. Welcome to the baffling world of inflation!

Inflation is a term that gets thrown around a lot, especially during tough economic times. But what really is inflation? It's simply the rate at which the general level of prices for goods and services rises, eroding your purchasing power. In other words, what you could buy for $1 a few years ago might cost $1.10 today. For many, this creeping sense of financial dread is all too real, making it feel like you're on a never-ending treadmill, running just to keep up with prices that seem to be racing ahead.

But here's the good news: you don't have to sit back and let inflation control your financial future! In **"Inflation Proof: 8 Smart Strategies to Keep Your Wallet Full,"** we'll explore practical, effective methods to fight back against inflation. This book is designed to be a friendly guide to help you navigate these murky waters with confidence and ease.

We'll break down complex concepts into doable practices that you can easily integrate into your life. From understanding budgets and smart investing to learning how to negotiate better prices and tapping into your creative skills for DIY projects, each chapter will provide you with tools to combat the challenges inflation presents.

Why is staying informed essential? Because knowledge is power! As you become more aware of economic trends, you can make informed decisions that will help you weather any financial storm. This isn't just about surviving; it's about thriving in an ever-changing world!

We'll also discuss the importance of diversifying your income streams. In today's gig economy, having a side hustle or two can be a game-changer. It not only provides you with extra cash but also gives you a safety net should you face unexpected expenses or job instability.

Throughout this book, we'll strike a friendly tone, keeping things light and accessible. This isn't a textbook filled with complicated jargon; it's a chat with a friend who genuinely wants to help. You'll find clear examples, relatable anecdotes, and action steps you can take immediately to start feeling more secure about your finances.

So, are you ready to take control of your finances? Strap in, because we're about to embark on a journey to not just survive inflation but to outsmart it at every turn. Let's dive in and explore the eight smart strategies to keep your wallet full!

Chapter 1:

Understanding Inflation: What It Is and Why It Matters

Inflation might sound like a highfalutin term that economists toss around in their fancy suits, but it's really not that complicated. Let's break it down into simple terms.

A Brief History of Inflation

Inflation has been around for as long as people have used money. Before cash, people traded goods directly—this is known as bartering. Imagine trading a basket of apples for a loaf of bread! But as societies evolved and money became the primary means of exchange, the idea of inflation started to take shape.

Throughout history, inflation has ebbed and flowed. During times of war, for example, governments often print more money to pay for military expenses. This can lead to inflation as the increased amount of money circulates while the supplies of goods and services remain the same or decrease. The classic example of runaway inflation is seen in places like Zimbabwe in the late 2000s, where prices skyrocketed overnight, and people needed wheelbarrows of cash to buy a loaf of bread!

What Causes Inflation?

There are a few primary reasons inflation happens:

1. **Demand-Pull Inflation**: This occurs when demand for goods and services outpaces supply. Picture a hot toy on Christmas. If everyone wants it but there aren't enough to go around, the price goes up!

2. **Cost-Push Inflation**: This happens when there's an increase in the cost of production. If the price of oil goes up, for instance, it becomes more expensive to transport goods. Companies then pass those costs onto consumers, resulting in higher prices.

3. **Built-In Inflation**: This is related to people's expectations. If workers expect prices to rise, they'll demand higher wages. If businesses pay those wages, they might raise prices to

maintain their profit margins, creating a cycle.

The Effects of Inflation

Inflation affects everyone—wage earners, retirees, businesses, and investors. When prices rise, your paycheck doesn't stretch as far, eroding your purchasing power. For retirees who rely on fixed incomes, this can be particularly painful.

While a moderate amount of inflation is normal and even healthy for an economy, high inflation can severely impact households. You might notice your grocery bills increasing, your rent going up, or everything from your morning coffee to your new shoes costing you more.

How to Measure Inflation

Inflation is measured using various indices, the most common being the Consumer Price

Index (CPI). The CPI tracks the prices of a predetermined basket of goods and services over time. When the cost of this basket goes up, that's a sign that inflation is happening.

Conclusion

Understanding inflation is the first step towards beating it. By knowing what causes it and how it can impact your financial life, you can begin to take the necessary steps to protect yourself. In the following chapters, we'll explore practical, actionable strategies that will empower you to counteract inflation and keep your wallet healthy. Whether it's through budgeting, investing smartly, or honing negotiation skills, there are plenty of ways to stay ahead of rising prices. So keep reading—we're just getting started!

Chapter 2:

Budgeting Basics: The First Step to Beating Inflation

When it comes to personal finance, there's one word that stands above the rest: **budgeting**. If you want to tackle inflation effectively, learning how to budget is essential. Let's dive deep into the world of budgeting and how it can help keep your financial health intact even when prices go up.

What is a Budget?

Simply put, a budget is a plan for your money. It helps you allocate your income towards different expenses and savings goals. Think of it as a roadmap for your finances. Without a budget, you might end up spending more than you make, and that can lead to debt—something that becomes even more burdensome when inflation strikes.

Setting Up Your Budget

<u>1. Assess Your Income</u>

Start by calculating your total monthly income. This includes your salary, bonuses, side gigs, or any other sources. Knowing exactly how much money you have coming in is crucial to understanding how much you can spend.

<u>2. Track Your Expenses</u>

For at least a month, keep track of all your expenses. This can be as simple as writing down every purchase you make or using an app that tracks spending automatically. Categorize your expenses into fixed and variable categories:

- **Fixed Expenses**: These are consistent monthly expenses, like rent, utilities, and insurance.
- **Variable Expenses**: These can change from month to month, including food, entertainment, and shopping.

3. Set Financial Goals

What do you want to accomplish financially? Your goals will help shape your budget. Short-term goals might include saving for a vacation, while long-term goals could be building an emergency fund or saving for retirement. Write down your goals and try to be specific, like, "I want to save $1,000 for a vacation by next summer."

4. Create Your Budget

Once you know your income and expenses, it's time to create your budget. Use a simple formula:

Income - Expenses = Savings/Surplus.

If your expenses are higher than your income, look for areas to cut back. Once you've created your budget, stick to it as closely as possible. Adjust it as needed, especially if you find certain expenses are consistently higher than anticipated.

Common Budgeting Methods

There are various budgeting methods you can use to find what works best for you:

- **50/30/20 Rule**: This guideline helps divide your income into three areas—50% for needs (like housing), 30% for wants (like dining out), and 20% for savings and debt repayment.

- **Zero-Based Budget**: In this method, every dollar of your income is allocated to specific expenses until you reach zero. If you have $2,000 in income, you'll assign every dollar to bills, savings, or debt repayment until there's nothing left.

- **Envelope System**: This is a more hands-on approach involving cash. You withdraw a set amount of cash for various categories (like groceries, entertainment, etc.) and place them in envelopes. Once the cash is gone from an envelope, you can't spend any more in that category until the next budget cycle.

Tips for Sticking to Your Budget

Sticking to a budget can be challenging, but here are some helpful tips:

- **Use Technology**: There are many budgeting apps available that can simplify the process. Look for one that suits your needs.

- **Review Regularly**: Check in on your budget regularly—weekly or monthly.

This allows you to see if you're on track and make adjustments if necessary.

- **Stay Motivated**: Keep your financial goals in mind. Remind yourself why you're budgeting and what you're working towards!

Making Adjustments in Inflationary Times

When inflation hits, it may mean you need to make some adjustments to your budget. You might find that food and gas prices have gone up, affecting your spending categories. Here's how to tackle it:

1. **Prioritize Needs Over Wants**: During inflationary times, re-evaluate your budget. Make sure you're covering all your essential expenses first.

2. **Cut Back on Discretionary Spending**: Find areas to reduce

spending, such as dining out or subscription services.

3. **Consider Substitutes**: If certain items have become too expensive, look for cheaper alternatives.

Conclusion

Mastering the art of budgeting is crucial for any financial strategy, especially when facing inflation. By systematically tracking your income and expenses and making informed choices about your money, you can reduce your stress and ensure that inflation does not derail your financial wellness. Remember, budgeting isn't about restriction; it's about being mindful of your choices and making them work for you!

Stay tuned for the next chapter, where we'll explore smart investing strategies that help your money grow—even when prices rise.

Chapter 3:

Smart Investing: Growing Your Money, Even When Prices Rise

Welcome to the exciting world of investing! A smart investment strategy isn't just about watching your money grow; it's about ensuring that inflation doesn't eat away at your savings. In this chapter, we're going to break down the essentials of investing, helping you to navigate this dynamic landscape confidently.

Why Invest?

Before we dive into the specifics, let's tackle the "why." Investing is essential because simply saving money can sometimes feel like running on a hamster wheel—especially during inflationary periods when the purchasing power of cash decreases. When you invest, your money can work for you, providing returns that can outpace inflation.

Types of Investments

There are many ways to invest your money. Here are some common types you might consider:

1. **Stocks**: Owning shares of a company gives you a stake in its success. Stocks have the potential for high returns but come with higher risk.

2. **Bonds**: When you buy a bond, you're lending money to an entity (like the government or a corporation) in exchange for interest payments. Bonds are generally considered safer than stocks but tend to offer lower returns.

3. **Real Estate**: Investing in property can provide rental income and is often considered a hedge against inflation, as property values tend to rise over time.

4. **Mutual Funds and ETFs**: These investment options allow you to pool

your money with other investors to buy a diversified portfolio of stocks or bonds. They offer a way to spread out risk.

5. **Commodities**: Investing in physical goods like gold, silver, or oil can act as a hedge against inflation, as commodity prices often rise during these periods.

Setting Investment Goals

Before you jump into investing, it's important to set clear goals:

- **Short-Term Goals**: These might include saving for a down payment on a house or a big trip, usually within three to five years.

- **Long-Term Goals**: These typically encompass retirement savings or funding your children's college education. Long-term investments can ride out market volatility.

Risk Tolerance

Understanding your risk tolerance is crucial when investing. Are you comfortable seeing the value of your investments fluctuate? If you're investing for the long haul, remember that markets will rise and fall; it's all part of the process.

Diversification: Your Best Friend

A key principle of investing is diversification—don't put all your eggs in one basket. By spreading your investments across various asset classes (stocks, bonds, real estate, etc.), you can reduce risk. If one investment performs poorly, others may do well, balancing out your returns.

Investing During Inflation

When inflation rises, certain investments perform better than others:

- **Stocks**: Historically, stocks can outperform inflation in the long run. Companies can raise their prices, thus increasing revenues.

- **Real Estate**: Property often appreciates in value during inflation, and rental income can also rise, making it a solid investment choice.

- **Commodities**: Precious metals like gold are often seen as safe bets during uncertain times, providing a hedge against inflation.

How to Start Investing

1. **Educate Yourself**: Read books, follow financial news, or consider taking a course to understand the basics of investing.

2. **Start Small**: You don't need a lot of money to begin investing—look for

platforms that allow you to start with a small amount.

3. **Consider a Financial Advisor**: If you're feeling overwhelmed, a financial advisor can help you create a personalized investment strategy tailored to your needs.

4. **Use Technology**: Numerous investment apps and platforms make it easier than ever to start investing, often with low fees.

Costs of Investing

Be sure to consider any fees associated with your investments. These can eat away at your returns. Look for low-fee investment options and always read the fine print.

Staying the Course

Investing is not an overnight win. The market may go up and down, but patience is key. Invest with a long-term perspective, and remember to review your portfolio regularly to ensure that it aligns with your goals.

Conclusion

Investing wisely can be your best tool in combating inflation and growing your wealth. By understanding the different types of investments, setting clear goals, and diversifying your portfolio, you can make informed decisions that will keep your wallet healthy even in tough economic times.

In the next chapter, we'll explore the art of haggling and negotiation—an invaluable skill that can save you money on countless purchases!

Chapter 4:

Haggling and Negotiation: Getting More for Less

Have you ever found yourself in a situation where you could have saved some money, if only you'd had the courage to ask for a better deal? Whether you're buying a car, haggling at a market, or negotiating with your utility provider, the ability to negotiate effectively is a powerful skill that can help you keep more money in your pocket.

Understanding the Art of Haggling

Haggling isn't just for flea markets or outdoor bazaars; it's a common practice in many types of shopping and service industries. While it might feel intimidating, a little preparation and confidence can go a long way.

Remember: Haggling is simply a conversation about value. It's not about trying to get something for nothing; it's about ensuring you feel good about what you're paying.

Preparing to Negotiate

Before you step into a negotiation, make sure you're ready. Here's how:

1. **Do Your Research**: Knowledge is powerful. Research the product or service's average price. Websites like Kelley Blue Book for cars or price comparison tools can help you understand what a fair price is.

2. **Know Your Budget**: Have a clear budget in mind before you start negotiating. This will help you stay within your limits and know when to walk away.

3. **Be Confident**: Confidence is key when negotiating. Stand tall, make eye contact, and speak clearly. Remember, the seller is also looking to make a sale, so you have leverage.

Strategies for Successful Negotiation

Here are some effective techniques to enhance your haggling skills:

1. **Start Low**: Offer a lower price than what you're willing to pay. This creates room for negotiation. For instance, if you're willing to pay $100 for a new jacket, you could start by offering $70.

2. **Listen Actively**: Pay attention to the seller's response. Listening carefully can give you insight into their position and help you craft better offers.

3. **Be Polite and Respectful**: Kindness can go a long way. Sellers are more

likely to work with you if you treat them with respect.

4. **Use Silence**: Sometimes, silence can be a powerful tool. After making an offer, pause and allow the seller to respond without filling the silence with nervous chatter.

5. **Be Willing to Walk Away**: If the deal isn't working for you, don't be afraid to walk away. This shows the seller you're serious about your limits. Sometimes, they might offer a better deal just to keep your business.

Negotiating in Different Settings

Different situations may require slightly different tactics. Here are some common scenarios where negotiation is beneficial:

1. **Buying a Car**: This is perhaps the most recognized area for negotiation. Salespeople expect you to haggle. Start

by discussing the vehicle's invoice price (what the dealer paid) rather than the sticker price.

2. **Renting an Apartment**: If you love a place but think the rent is too high, try negotiating for a lower price, especially if you have good credit and can demonstrate you'll be a reliable tenant.

3. **Utility Bills**: Sometimes, you can negotiate your rate with service providers. Call them up, express your concerns about rising costs, and ask if they can offer any discounts or changes to your plan.

4. **Freelance Services**: If you're hiring a freelancer or contractor, don't be afraid to ask if they can adjust their rates or provide a package deal that meets your budget.

Practicing Your Skills

Just like any other skill, negotiating gets easier with practice. Start small at places where haggling is expected—like flea markets or yard sales. You can also practice negotiation with friends or family members to build your confidence.

Conclusion

Haggling and negotiation are invaluable skills that can empower you to save money in a world where prices are constantly rising due to inflation. By preparing effectively, practicing your techniques, and maintaining a positive attitude, you can make every dollar count.

Next, we'll explore how DIY solutions can further help you cut costs and keep more money in your pocket!

Chapter 5:

DIY Solutions: Cutting Costs With Your Skills

Let's face it: sometimes, life gets expensive. Between bills, groceries, and unexpected expenses, it can feel like your wallet is perpetually emptying. But what if you could cut some costs by tapping into your skills? Welcome to the world of DIY (do-it-yourself)!

What is DIY?

DIY refers to creating, building, or repairing things yourself instead of hiring someone else to do it. This can range from home improvements and car maintenance to crafting gifts or creating useful household items. The best part? It saves you money while giving you a sense of accomplishment!

Why DIY?

1. **Cost Savings**: Hiring professionals can be expensive. By doing things yourself, you can save a significant amount of money.

2. **Learning New Skills**: DIY projects are a fantastic way to learn something new. You may discover hidden talents and hobbies along the way!

3. **Personal Satisfaction**: Completing a DIY project can be incredibly rewarding. You get to see your hard work come to life, and it can boost your creativity.

4. **Customization**: When you create something yourself, you can tailor it to your tastes and preferences.

Popular DIY Projects

Let's take a look at some common DIY projects that can help you save money around the house.

1. Home Repairs

Instead of calling a handyman for small repairs, try tackling them yourself. Things like fixing leaky faucets, painting rooms, or changing light fixtures can be done with a little research and effort. There are tons of online videos and tutorials available to guide you through almost any repair project!

2. Gardening

Creating your own vegetable or herb garden can save you money on groceries. Even if you have limited space, consider container gardening, where you can grow plants in pots on a balcony or patio. Fresh veggies and herbs not only taste better but also cut down on your shopping expenses.

3. Upcycling Furniture

Instead of buying new furniture, consider upcycling what you already have. A little paint, some new hardware, or creative reupholstering can breathe new life into old pieces. Not only is this budget-friendly, but it also allows you to create unique items for your home.

4. Homemade Cleaning Products

Instead of purchasing expensive cleaning supplies, try making your own. Most effective cleaners can be made with simple ingredients like vinegar, baking soda, and essential oils. Not only are these DIY cleaners cheaper, but they're often healthier for you and the environment, too!

5. Crafting Gifts

Instead of buying gifts for friends and family, consider making something special. Handmade gifts, whether it's a knitted scarf, custom photo book, or homemade candles, add a personal touch that store-bought items often lack.

How to Get Started with DIY

1. **Identify Projects**: Consider areas where you spend money regularly. Can some of those expenses be eliminated by doing it yourself?
2. **Learn and Research**: Read articles, watch video tutorials, or take local workshops to learn about the projects you want to try.
3. **Gather Supplies**: Make a list of what you need. Check your home for items you can repurpose, and see if you can borrow tools before buying new ones.
4. **Start Small**: If you're new to DIY, start with simple projects that don't require extensive skills. This will help build your confidence.

Tips for Successful DIY

- **Be Prepared**: Have all your materials ready before you begin a project to ensure a smooth process.

- **Take Your Time**: Rushing through a project may lead to mistakes, so take your time to do it right.

- **Don't Be Afraid to Fail**: Not every DIY project will turn out perfectly—and that's okay! Learn from your mistakes and improve with each project.

Resources for DIY

Here are some great resources to consider:

- **Online Platforms**: Websites like YouTube, Pinterest, and DIY blogs are filled with ideas and step-by-step instructions for countless DIY projects.

- **Community Classes**: Many local community centers offer workshops for skills like woodworking, crafting, painting, and more. This can be a great way to learn alongside others.

- **Books and Magazines**: Look for DIY guides or home improvement magazines at your local library or bookstore. These often provide inspiration and detailed how-to guides.

Conclusion

DIY projects are a fantastic way to cut costs while also taking pride in your accomplishments. From home repairs and gardening to crafting personalized gifts, the sky's the limit when it comes to what you can achieve on your own. By embracing your creativity and willingness to learn, you can significantly reduce your expenses. Plus, think of all the skills you'll gain along the way!

In the next chapter, we'll take a closer look at smart saving strategies and where to put your money amidst rising inflation. Let's keep that wallet healthy!

Chapter 6:

Saving Wisely: Where to Put Your Money Amid Inflation

As inflation rises, the need for careful saving and smart financial strategies becomes ever more crucial. Understanding where to put your money can mean the difference between just getting by and building wealth over time. In this chapter, we'll dive into effective saving strategies and explore the best options for keeping your hard-earned dollars safe and growing.

The Importance of Saving

At its core, saving is about preparing for the unexpected and making opportunities for the future. Life can throw curveballs—

unexpected medical bills, car repairs, or job losses. Having savings gives you a financial cushion that allows you to navigate such challenges without falling into debt.

Types of Savings Accounts

When considering where to put your money, not all savings accounts are created equal. Here are some common types you should know about:

1. Regular Savings Account

A regular savings account at your bank or credit union is a basic choice for saving. These accounts typically offer lower interest rates but provide easy access to your funds. They're great for short-term savings or an emergency fund.

2. High-Yield Savings Account

High-yield savings accounts offer higher interest rates compared to traditional savings accounts. They may require you to maintain a minimum balance or limit the number of withdrawals. This is a smart choice if you want to earn more on your saved funds without taking on the risk associated with investing.

3. Money Market Accounts

Money market accounts often offer higher interest rates and come with check-writing privileges. However, they typically require a higher minimum balance than regular savings accounts. They offer a good mix of saving and liquidity, allowing you to earn interest while keeping your money accessible.

4. Certificates of Deposit (CDs)

CDs require you to lock away your money for a specified term (ranging from a few months to several years) in exchange for a higher interest rate. They're safe and guaranteed but come with penalties for early withdrawal. If you're sure you won't need access to your cash for a while, CDs can be a smart choice for higher returns.

Building an Emergency Fund

One of the first savings goals you should consider is building an emergency fund. An emergency fund is designed to cover unexpected expenses, such as medical bills or urgent home repairs. Here are some tips on how to build one:

1. **Target Amount**: Aim for three to six months' worth of expenses. This figure should cover your essential costs, allowing you to live without income for a short period.

2. **Set It Aside**: Open a dedicated savings account for your emergency fund. This helps to keep it separate from your everyday spending.

3. **Automate Savings**: Set up automatic transfers from your checking to your savings account. Treat your savings like a regular expense to ensure you consistently contribute.

4. **Start Small and Build**: If saving several months' worth of expenses seems daunting, start with a smaller target, such as $500 or $1,000. As you reach each milestone, increase your goal.

Smart Saving Strategies

Here are a few strategies to maximize your savings in an era of rising inflation:

1. **Use Coupons and Cashback Apps**: Take advantage of coupons, discounts, and apps that offer cashback on your purchases. This can help stretch your budget and allow you to save more.

2. **Set Specific Savings Goals**: Whether it's a vacation, a new car, or a down payment for a house, having specific goals can motivate you to save. Break these goals into smaller, manageable chunks to track your progress.

3. **Review and Adjust Monthly Expenses**: Regularly review your budget and look for ways to cut back on non-essential spending. Every little bit adds up!

4. **Consider Savings Bonds**: U.S. savings bonds are government-backed and relatively low-risk. They can be a good option for longer-term savings, though they may not provide the best short-term returns.

Staying Informed About Interest Rates

Keep an eye on the interest rates being offered by various financial institutions. As inflation rises, the Federal Reserve may adjust interest rates, impacting the rates offered on savings accounts and investment vehicles. Stay informed and be ready to move your money to get the best returns.

Conclusion

Smart saving is essential in navigating inflation and ensuring you thrive financially. By using the right savings accounts, setting realistic goals, and adopting strategic saving techniques, you can build a robust financial foundation. Review your savings goals regularly, adapt to economic changes, and watch your financial security grow!

In our next chapter, we will explore income diversification and how tapping into multiple revenue streams can enhance your financial resilience during inflationary times. Don't miss it!

Chapter 7:

Income Diversification: Finding Extra Dollars in Unexpected Places

In today's fast-paced world, relying on a single source of income is no longer enough for many people. The economic climate is unpredictable, making income diversification an essential aspect of financial stability. This chapter will explore various ways to diversify your income streams, providing you with strategies to enhance your financial security amidst the challenges of inflation.

What is Income Diversification?

Income diversification refers to having multiple streams of income rather than depending solely on one job or source of revenue. By diversifying your income, you spread risk and increase your financial resilience. If one source decreases, others can help fill the gap.

Why is Income Diversification Important?

1. **Financial Security**: Multiple income streams provide a safety net, reducing pressure on your primary job and offering peace of mind.

2. **Increased Earnings Potential**: With diverse income sources, you can increase your overall earnings and build wealth more effectively.

3. **Skill Development**: Pursuing additional income streams often means learning new skills and exploring different areas of interest, leading to personal and professional growth.

4. **Resilience to Inflation**: When inflation rises, costs associated with living increase. By having diverse

income streams, you can better cope with these rising expenses.

Exploring Income Diversification Options

Now that we understand the importance of income diversification, let's explore some ideas for increasing your income:

1. Side Hustles

One of the most popular ways to diversify income is by starting a side hustle. This can take many forms, depending on your skills and interests:

- **Freelancing**: If you have skills in writing, graphic design, web development, or social media management, consider freelancing platforms like Upwork or Fiverr.

- **Ride-Sharing/Delivery**: Companies like Uber, Lyft, DoorDash, or

Postmates offer flexible opportunities to earn money using your vehicle.

- **Tutoring**: If you excel in particular subjects, consider offering tutoring services, either locally or online through platforms like Tutor.com.

2. Passive Income Sources

Passive income involves earning money with minimal active effort. While it may take time to set up, it can provide ongoing revenue:

- **Rental Income**: Investing in real estate can generate rental income. Ensure you conduct thorough research to understand the housing market before diving in.

- **Investing in Dividend Stocks**: Some companies offer dividends, a portion of profits paid to shareholders. By investing in these stocks, you can receive regular payments.

- **Creating Digital Products**: If you have expertise in a particular area, consider creating e-books, online courses, or other digital products that can sell repeatedly.

3. Starting a Small Business

If you have a passion or hobby you love, consider turning it into a small business. This could be anything from baking and selling goods, crafting handmade items, to offering consulting services in a field you know well.

4. Investing in Your Education and Skills

One of the most valuable things you can do for your future earning potential is to invest in your education and skills. Consider taking courses to gain new certifications or develop skills that could open the door to higher-paying jobs.

Tips for Successfully Diversifying Your Income

1. **Start Small**: If you're new to side hustles or investing, start small. Pick one additional income source to focus on initially.

2. **Time Management**: Be sure to balance your time effectively between your primary job and your side income. Organize and prioritize tasks to avoid burnout.

3. **Networking**: Connect with others in your desired field. Networking can lead to new opportunities, clients, and partnerships.

4. **Stay Informed**: Keep an eye on trends in your area of interest. Understanding market demand can help you make informed decisions about where to invest time and resources.

5. **Review and Adjust**: Regularly assess your income sources to determine what is working and what isn't. Adjust your strategies based on your experiences and changing circumstances.

Conclusion

Diversifying your income is a smart financial strategy that provides greater security and resilience, especially during inflationary times. Exploring side hustles, passive income sources, and small business opportunities allows you to create multiple revenue streams. Investing time in your education and building a robust network can further enhance your earnings potential.

In the next chapter, we'll emphasize the importance of staying informed about economic trends and how keeping up with changes can empower you to make better financial decisions. Stay tuned!

Chapter 8:

Staying Informed: Keeping Up with Economic Trends

In a world that changes as quickly as ours, staying informed about economic trends is crucial for personal finance success. Whether it's understanding inflation rates, shifts in job markets, or investment opportunities, knowledge empowers you to make smart financial decisions. In this chapter, we'll explore how to stay informed and why it matters for your financial health.

The Importance of Staying Informed

1. **Making Informed Decisions**: Understanding economic trends allows

you to make educated decisions about spending, saving, and investing.

2. **Identifying Opportunities**: The economy is always evolving. By being aware of changes, you can identify opportunities for growth and success.

3. **Preparing for Challenges**: Economic downturns, rising inflation, and job market shifts can catch you off guard. Staying informed helps you anticipate and prepare for such challenges.

4. **Enhancing Financial Literacy**: The more you learn, the more financially literate you become. This knowledge can give you greater confidence in managing your finances.

How to Stay Informed About Economic Trends

1. **Follow the News**: Tune in to reputable news sources for updates on the

economy, job markets, and inflation. Look for financial news from sources like Bloomberg, CNBC, or The Wall Street Journal.

2. **Use Financial Apps**: Many apps provide timely information about stock prices, economic indicators, and investment opportunities. Consider apps like Robinhood or Acorns to get started.

3. **Subscribe to Newsletters**: Financial newsletters can provide curated information on market trends, investment strategies, and economic forecasts. Look for ones that match your interests.

4. **Engage in Discussions**: Chat with friends, family, or financial advisors about current events and economic trends. Discussing your thoughts and

concerns can provide valuable perspectives and insights.

5. **Participate in Forums or Groups**: Online forums (like Reddit's personal finance section) can be great for discussing trends with others. They often offer diverse opinions and resources for learning.

6. **Continual Learning**: Consider enrolling in finance or economics courses, either in-person or online. Platforms like Coursera and Khan Academy offer free resources that can boost your financial literacy.

Making Sense of Information

With so much information available, it can be overwhelming. Here's how to filter and make sense of it:

1. **Identify Reliable Sources**: Always cross-check information from multiple

trusted sources. Mark reputable sites or authors you rely on for accurate insights.

2. **Stay Skeptical**: Be cautious about news headlines that seem too good to be true. Always dig deeper to understand the broader context.

3. **Follow Trends, Not Noise**: Focus on data and trends that impact your financial life relevantly. Short-lived news cycles may distract you from more meaningful shifts happening in the economy.

4. **Take Notes**: Keeping notes or a personal financial journal can help solidify what you learn and allow for reflection on how it affects your financial strategy.

Conclusion

Staying informed about economic trends is vital to navigating your financial journey successfully. Knowing how to seek out and understand this information allows you to make better decisions and seize opportunities even in times of uncertainty. Remember, the goal is not just to know what's happening in the economy but to use that knowledge to empower your financial future.

Throughout this book, we've discussed eight smart strategies to beat inflation, from budgeting and investing to negotiating and embracing DIY projects. Now, you're equipped with tools and knowledge to navigate inflation and maintain financial health, setting the stage for a secure future.

Thank you for joining me. May your journey towards financial wellness be rewarding and fulfilling!

www.ingramcontent.com/pod-product-compliance
Lightning Source LLC
Chambersburg PA
CBHW070415230526
45471CB00006B/2808